HERALDRY

John Martin Robinson

HERALDRY

Chatto & Windus
LONDON

Published in 1989 by
Chatto & Windus Ltd
30 Bedford Square
London WC1B 3SG

A CIP catalogue record for this book
is available from the British Library.

ISBN 0 7011 3559 X

Photoset and printed in Great Britain by
Redwood Burn Limited, Trowbridge, Wiltshire

CONTENTS

ACKNOWLEDGEMENTS

I am most grateful to the following for assistance
– especially for help in obtaining appropriate illustrations:

British Tourist Authority
Stephen Croad and the staff at the N.M.R.
Philip Davies
Donald Findlay
Howard Frith
Greater London Record Office
Mrs Margaret Lancaster
Jeremy Lewis
The Duke of Norfolk, Earl Marshal
Alec Peever
Alan Powers
RIBA Library
Mrs Ian Rodger
Gavin Stamp
Reece Winstone
Thomas Woodcock, Somerset Herald of Arms
York City Council
Robert Yorke, Archivist to the College of Arms

JUSTITIA REGINA VIRTUTUM

INTRODUCTION

All cities, most towns and many villages in England can show examples of the use of decorative heraldry on public and private buildings, gateways, shop fronts and street furniture, while heraldic pub signs are so frequently encountered as almost to be taken for granted. This lavish display of heraldry is a particular feature of English traditional urban design, though it is not unique to this country. In Rome, for instance, all the major churches have painted cartouches of the arms of the Pope, John Paul II, and of their appropriate cardinal. In Spain the royal arms of King Juan Carlos are displayed on all public buildings, while the most impressive displays of historic architectural heraldry anywhere in Europe can be found in Toledo and Salamanca. In England, however, the decorative and architectural uses of heraldry have been developed more consistently and comprehensively than anywhere else. Indeed, England can make a good claim to have in vented the use of heraldry as part of the permanent vocabulary of architecture in the first place rather than as a form of temporary decoration or pageantry. The display of well-designed heraldic devices adds greatly to the attractions of the average English town, and is a tradition worth encouraging and developing. It is one of the many advantages of living in a fully-fledged monarchy.

The purely decorative and architectural use of heraldry can be traced back to the middle of the thirteenth century, about a hundred years after the emergence of heraldry itself. Heraldry, defined as the system-atic hereditary use of an arrangement of charges or devices on a shield, first appeared at about the same moment over a wide area of western Europe in the mid-twelfth century. Between 1135 and 1155, seals show the general adoption of heraldic devices in England, France, Germany,

Spain and Italy. There has been much debate about the origins of heraldry, but the subject remains obscure and no definite or totally convincing theory has been put forward to explain how it came into being. Heraldry in its early stages certainly had strong military associations. The traditional explanation is that the original reason for the display of arms on shields was to enable knights in armour to be identified on the battlefield. This would not, however, have been a very practical means of identification in the *melée* of hand-to-hand combat. It seems more likely that from the very beginning heraldry was a form of personal display. It was a subjective demonstration on the part of individual knights, a form of vanity, rather than a practical military device. The feudal social and military order of the twelfth century was such that, once invented, coats of arms found a ready market as status symbols, and were popularized by the tournament rather than by real warfare. The tournament, which also emerged at that time, was a form of stylized mock combat between knights developed as a form of training in the use of arms and as an entertainment. It soon became highly organized and hedged around with rules and elaborate pageantry, of which heraldry became an integral part. The knights involved in the combat wore their individual arms on their shields, on painted linen surcoats over their armour (coats of arms), on their horse trappings and their crest on their helmets (modelled out of wood and vellum, painted and gilded), while the surrounding lists, barriers and stands might also be decorated with painted shields of the arms and colours of the combatants, rather in the way that the colours of rival teams are used to differentiate 'the fans' at modern football matches.

From being used as a form of temporary decoration in this way at tournaments, it was only a short step to the display of heraldry elsewhere. It seems that the next phase in the decorative use of heraldry may have been taken in Paris, the source of inspiration for many developments in early medieval art, architecture and decoration. At a banquet given in the great hall of the Temple at Paris in 1254, King Louis IX of France hung the walls for the occasion with painted wooden shields bearing the arms of the great nobles of France, thus adapting the trappings of a tournament to make a form of internal embellishment. One of the guests at the banquet was King Henry III of England, who was so impressed by what he saw that he at once adopted the idea himself. Henry III had a passion for heraldry, and immediately grasped the point of the French king's novel decorations. Henry was himself a great builder and patron of the arts, the greatest among English medieval monarchs. He was responsible for extending or rebuilding and decorating a large number of castles, palaces and chapels. His *magnum opus*, and favourite project, was the rebuilding of Westminster Abbey on the grandest scale and in the most up-to-date French Gothic style.

Even before his visit to France, Henry had made use of coats of arms to adorn metalwork, tiles and painted wall decoration. As early as 1237, for instance, he had commissioned a silver platter ornamented with the Royal Arms as a present for the Queen. In 1240 he ordered his arms to be painted on the window shutters of his Great Chamber at the Tower of London, and in 1266 extended the practice to all the doors and shutters of the New Hall and Chamber at Winchester Castle. The Great Hall at Rochester Castle and the chapel at Havering were likewise embellished with heraldic stained glass at about the same time. The latter depicted not just Henry's own arms, but also those of his father-in-law, the Count of Provence. And in 1268 Henry instructed the Keeper of the Works at Westminster to send to the palace at Havering twenty glass windows decorated with forty shields of arms for the Queen's Chamber. At Westminster Abbey the floor of the Chapter House had been decorated with heraldry *circa* 1253, and the floor tiles of the Westminster Chapter House have the earliest surviving decorative representation of the King's Arms. The visit to Paris, however, gave him the idea for a more architectural form of heraldic decoration, by copying the example of Louis IX, not in temporary painted wood but in permanent carved stone.

In 1258 he ordered that the spandrels of the aisle arcades at Westminster Abbey should be adorned with carved stone shields representing his own arms and those of the Royal houses with which he was connected by marriage, viz. the arms of Edward the Confessor, of England, the Empire, France, Provence and Scotland, together with those of his principal vassals, the great English Barons: Clare, Bigod, Montfort, Warenne, Bohun, Arundel, de Quency, de Lacy, Richard Earl of Cornwall (and one unidentified). When coloured, these shields must have made a grand display of royal and baronial glory, and the idea soon came to be widely copied elsewhere, both inside and outside buildings, as the Sovereign's example was emulated by the barons and

WESTMINSTER ABBEY The choir aisles of Westminster Abbey have the earliest heraldic architectural decoration in Europe. The carved stone shields of arms in the spandrels of the arches were inspired by temporary painted wooden decorations at tournaments and were here adapted by Henry III to form part of the permanent decoration of the abbey church. This started a fashion that was soon copied in the interior and exterior of buildings throughout the land. These two shields show the arms of the King of France *semy with fleurs de lys Or* and of the Holy Roman Emperor with an *eagle displayed*.

great ecclesiastics. By the end of the thirteenth century heraldry had come to be a standard part of the decoration of castles, churches, palaces, houses and tombs.

This can be seen as an aspect of the growth of courtly romanticism at that time and a manifestation of the more secular trends of the age; heraldry taking some of the place hitherto occupied by religious symbolism. Within a short time coats of arms became the standard form of embellishment on Gothic buildings – at first modestly, and then with increasing elaboration and decorative fancy as the Middle Ages progressed. Heraldry provided the artist and architect with an easy repertory of ready-made motifs, as well as providing the client with a satisfactory way of stamping his personality on his building projects and property.

The development of heraldry as a form of artistic and architectural embellishment in the late thirteenth century received a further fillip from Edward I's military ideals and cult of chivalry. In Edward's reign the whole of court life seems to have been touched by a romantic glamour reflected in rich pageantry, new ceremonial and the general

WARKWORTH CASTLE, NORTH-UMBERLAND Percy heraldry on the Lion Tower including a large Percy lion, shield of *lozenges* and helmet with lion crest, *circa* 1400. This magnificent medieval display of family heraldry, here marking the entrance to the great hall of the castle, was the inspiration for many similar Victorian schemes.

elaboration of heraldry. This was a European-wide development at the time, but the impact probably went deeper in England than in other countries, and the use of heraldic decoration was sometimes taken to extremes. The canopy over the tomb of Edward Crouchback in Westminster Abbey, for instance, was painted with no fewer than 150 coats of arms, while the gatehouse of Kirkham Priory (built in 1300) in Yorkshire was entirely covered with the arms of the founders and benefactors of the Priory, and at Butley Priory in Suffolk the coats of arms adorning the gatehouse filled no fewer than seven closely packed rows, like a sheet of postage stamps. The decorative fancy and exquisite craftsmanship of late thirteenth-century heraldic art is seen in its most fully developed form in the Eleanor Crosses which Edward erected to commemorate the funeral procession of his wife Eleanor of Castile, who died in Nottinghamshire in 1290. Her twelve-day funeral journey from Harby to Westminster Abbey was given a permanent memorial in the form of a stone cross at each place where the coffin rested overnight. Each of them was decorated on the sides with shields of the arms of England and Castile, as can be seen still on the surviving examples at Geddington and Hardingstone in Northamptonshire and Waltham Cross in Essex. That at Charing Cross itself is a Victorian copy, designed by E. M. Barry to replace the original, destroyed by the Cromwellians in the Civil War.

The cult of the pageantry of death and the employment of heraldry for the purpose also had its origins in France; Edward I in his plans for the commemoration of his wife being influenced by the pomp and circumstance that had surrounded the return of the body of St. Louis of France from Tunis to the Abbey of St. Denis. The stations of the last stages of the funeral procession of St. Louis had been marked by similar ceremonial and the erection of stone crosses known as the Montjoies of St. Louis.

Though this kind of ceremonial funeral with permanent heraldic display reached its apogee in the later Middle Ages, the fashion lingered on in a reduced form into the seventeenth, eighteenth and nineteenth centuries, in the habit of displaying a hatchment of the arms

GLASTONBURY, SOMERSET, GEORGE HOTEL, HIGH STREET Originally built as a pilgrims' inn for Glastonbury Abbey *circa* 1470, it is a remarkable survival of a late Perpendicular secular building. Over the entrance archway are three original shields of arms depicting the abbey's heraldry with the royal arms of Edward IV, in whose reign the inn was built. The use of heraldic shields to ornament Perpendicular stone panels of important architectural features was an almost standard feature of the late Gothic style, secular as well as religious, and the inspiration for Pugin's heraldic decoration on the Palace of Westminster.

of the deceased for a year after his death over the front door of his residence. This still occurs from time to time at the occasional Oxford college when the head dies in office, and is a custom which could well be revived on a more widespread scale. Such hatchments, after being displayed for a year on the house, were then deposited in the local church. Many dating from the eighteenth and nineteenth centuries are a familiar sight, hanging aloft diamond-wise in the old parish churches and family chapels of England; they are painted on square wooden boards or canvas with simple black frames. Where the deceased was married, his arms are shown impaled with those of his wife, and if the widow outlived him, only the half behind the deceased's arms is painted black, the background of his living spouse being painted white.

In the fourteenth and fifteenth centuries, the architectural manifestation of heraldry became increasingly standardized and uniform. In churches, coats of arms and crests embellished corbels, the bosses of the vaults, stained glass in the windows, the spandrels of arches, the panels of screens and tomb chests. In houses, colleges and secular buildings it also became the norm to have a grand heraldic display over the gatehouse, on oriel windows and the metal vanes of the roof, as well as finials of single heraldic beasts on gables and parapets, as can be seen in the colleges at Oxford or Cambridge. The architectural use of heraldry in Gothic architecture reached its ultimate prominence in the decoration of King's College Chapel at Cambridge. There, all the stone carving is devoted to uninhibited dynastic display on the part of the new Tudor monarchy; there is no religious imagery in the stonework at all; everywhere six-foot high rampant greyhounds and dragons support the Royal Arms. Immense and deeply undercut Tudor roses and Beaufort portcullises are set off against the bare Perpendicular stone panelling.

Stained-glass windows in particular formed an excellent vehicle for heraldic display, the patterns and colours of coats of arms lending themselves well to glazing. Surviving medieval stained glass such as that in York Minster contains much elaborate heraldic decoration; the windows in the Chapter House, for instance, contain royal arms in medallions, including the *fleurs de lys* of France, the castles of Castile and the chalices of Galicia, while the nave windows have borders displaying the arms of the royal and noble benefactors of the Minster and of the great northern families. The display of heraldry in stained glass, both in secular and religious buildings, has continued to be one of the most popular uses of heraldry down to the present day, though it reached the most elaborate levels of perfection in the Tudor and again in the Victorian periods. Though it can be seen from the exterior, especially at night when it is lit up from the inside, it is best seen looking out, with the patterns and colours silhouetted and enriched by sunlight.

In the late sixteenth and seventeenth centuries, there was a certain diminution in the use of heraldry in architecture. The Renaissance brought with it a new vocabulary of Italian classical decoration which ousted the more Gothic excesses associated with the architectural use of heraldry in the late Middle Ages. Heraldry tended to be once more associated with temporary decorations for royal and other pageantry rather than permanently executed in stone. Thus, for the marriage of

Prince Arthur to Catherine of Aragon in 1501 very elaborate wooden and canvas arches were erected, embellished with paintings of the Royal Arms, badges, devices and supporters. And these temporary arches and other forms of 'stage scenery' in the streets of London became a standard item of royal ceremonial at coronations, marriages, receptions for foreign dignitaries and so forth. Because of their flimsy nature, no architectural heraldic street decorations of this type have survived, but their character is reflected in structures like pumps, conduits, fountains and market crosses often embellished with the arms of a town, corporation or particular benefactor, as in the case of Hobson's Conduit (1614) at Cambridge and Carfax Conduit, Oxford (though the latter was removed to the grounds of Nuneham Courtenay in the eighteenth century to serve as a garden ornament). The heraldic decoration of gateways also continued to be a feature of 'Gothic Survival' buildings, often reaching a climax in the Elizabethan and Jacobean frontispieces of new college or university buildings at Oxford and Cambridge.

The rule tended to be, however, that the more strictly classical the design of a building, the less use was made of heraldry on its elevation. In the seventeenth century, heraldry played little or no part in the decoration of the houses and palaces of Inigo Jones or Wren, for instance. Even Vanbrugh, who was himself a herald (first of all Carlisle Herald Extraordinary and then Clarenceux King of Arms), made little use of heraldic devices in his buildings. In the eighteenth century, heraldry was usually confined on the outside of Palladian-style build-ings to the embellishment of pediments, and was strictly contained by the overall discipline of the classical architecture. A good example is the display of the Devonshire arms in the pediment over the entrance to the stables designed by James Paine at Chatsworth in 1758. There, the life-size stone stags supporting the Cavendish arms have real antlers. Heraldic devices were also used to decorate classical friezes. Where the frieze is Doric, for example, the family or corporate crest is often used for the metopes between the triglyphs, an excellent example of the integration of heraldry into routine architectural vocabulary.

CHATSWORTH, DERBYSHIRE The stable block designed by James Paine in 1758–63 for William Cavendish, 4th Duke of Devonshire, is a superb example of second generation Anglo-Palladian architecture. As in the case of many buildings of this type and date, the use of heraldry is restricted to a cartouche within the pediment, and is strictly confined by the overall classical design of the architecture. The stone stags supporting the Cavendish arms are life-size and have real antlers. This splendid achievement was carved by Henry Watson, a Derbyshire craftsman whose bill for this work is preserved in the Chatsworth muniment room.

The most common appearance of heraldry in the street in the eighteenth century was, however, much less elevated. It was generally used to decorate shop fronts. Apart from the fact that many tradesmen were employed in purveying heraldic decoration in the form of coach painting with the family arms, or engraving crests on silver and such like, and naturally wished to display their wares, they also liked to put up on their shops, as a form of advertisement, the arms of noble or royal patrons, a practice which survives in the twentieth century in the display of royal warrants on those shops in London which are recognized by the Lord Chamberlain as official purveyors of particular goods to the Royal Household.

The granting of royal warrants, betokening services to the Sovereign and members of his family or household, dates back to the Middle Ages but gathered momentum in the reign of Elizabeth I. Betty Whittington's *Short History of the Royal Warrant* (1961) charts this development and records the wide variety of trades concerned. It was only in the eighteenth century, however, that the Royal Arms began to be regularly displayed by tradesmen, and though no early examples survive, many are recorded in drawings, watercolours and engravings. The majority of 'By appointment' shopkeepers flourished in the cities of London and Westminster, and some late Georgian examples of the Royal Arms do still survive on old shop fronts there, including the former Savory and Moore chemist's shop front in Bond Street and Floris, the perfumers, in Jermyn Street, though those on Freibourg and Treyer, the tobacconists, in the Haymarket have disappeared, alas, in

LONDON, FLORIS, JERMYN STREET
This early nineteenth-century perfumer's shop front retains the royal arms of George IV in Coade stone. This was a standard design used both in churches, such as Christ Church, Spitalfields, and on shops as a royal warrant. Floris is a rare survival of the display of heraldry on Georgian shops, once a common feature of the streets of London and other towns.

recent years. But royal tradesmen were by no means confined to London. Cheltenham, Bath, Tunbridge Wells, Brighton and Weymouth all have shops still displaying the late Georgian Royal Arms, recording the patronage of George III and George IV, and more recent examples can be found in Windsor, King's Lynn, Aberdeen and Ballater, the towns serving Windsor Castle, Sandringham and Balmoral Castle.

Royal warrants in the eighteenth century were granted under oath and by the Board of the Green Cloth, but as the number of shopkeepers patronized by the royal family proliferated, the organization was revised in the nineteenth century. Queen Victoria and Prince Albert overhauled the whole system. The granting of royal warrants then passed to the office of the Lord Chamberlain who was given ultimate control, aided by the advice of the Royal Household Tradesmen's Warrants Committee and the professional assistance of the Royal Warrant Holders' Association which keeps a list of the recommended firms for producing approved versions of the Royal Arms in different media for display on shop fronts.

In 1907, Edward VII tightened the system further, granting a charter to the Warrant Holders' Association and restricting the display of warrants to the arms of the Sovereign, Sovereign's consort and the heir to the throne only. Previously, other members of the Royal Family had granted warrants, but this is no longer the case. Although a royal warrant lapses on the death of the grantor, the courtesy of using the phrase 'By appointment to His or Her Late Majesty' is extended to the grantee. But following recent legislation such firms are forbidden from displaying the arms after a certain time. This proves a threat to the appearance of many old-established shops, where a group of consecutive warrants adds greatly to their aura of distinction, as in the case of Trumpers' barber's shop in Curzon Street, the window of which displays arms of different members of the Royal Family over a period of seventy or eighty years.

Today, rather less than a thousand traders and firms enjoy the privilege of displaying the Royal Arms, and wherever they appear they

LONDON, G.F. TRUMPER, CURZON STREET, MAYFAIR This barber's shop retains a resolutely Edwardian image, and its shop front displays a cumulative series of royal warrants on glass covering a period of over seventy years. The right to display the arms of deceased monarchs was withdrawn in 1978, but it is to be hoped that old-established displays of this type will not be affected.

enhance the general street scene, being a notable feature of Savile Row, Bond Street, Knightsbridge and other fashionable West End locations. It seems rather a pity that heraldic tradesmen's warrants are now restricted mainly to royal ones. It is a rare pleasure to come across surviving noblemen's warrants, including the Duke of Norfolk's on a jeweller's shop in Sheffield and a chemist's shop in Glossop, or the Duke of Westminster's on a tailor's in Chester.

As the architectural display of heraldry increased in popularity in the Middle Ages, so heraldry itself became more elaborate. When they first emerged in the twelfth century, shields of arms had comprised simple, usually geometrical designs in restricted colours, but by the late thirteenth century they had become much richer and increasingly complex in design with the introduction of a number of fabulous and chimerical creatures, and patterns which moved far away from the

LONDON, THE COLLEGE OF ARMS, QUEEN VICTORIA STREET Incorporated by Richard III in 1484, the College of Arms has occupied its present site since 1555. Destroyed in the Great Fire, it was rebuilt in 1688. It houses the official body responsible for all aspects of heraldry in England and Wales. The college arms are visible in the overthrow of the gate and on the Victorian porch beyond. During the day, a heraldic banner is also flown from the porch depicting the arms of the officer in waiting for that week, each of the heralds and pursuivants serving in a rota to deal with heraldic and genealogical business.

LONDON, THE COLLEGE OF ARMS The College occupies the site of Derby House, the medieval town house of the Stanleys, Earls of Derby, and the two plaques in the courtyard display heraldry related to that family. Though dating from the 1680s, it is almost certain that these carved panels were copied from similar decorations on the previous building and are a rare indication of how heraldry might have been displayed on the town house of a great medieval nobleman. (Since this photograph, the royal supporters – a lion and unicorn – have been moved to the main entrance steps.)

simple vigorous geometry of early days. A development, originating in Spain and first seen in England in the arms of Eleanor of Castile, wife of Edward I, was the incorporation of other quarterings of arms inherited via heraldic heiresses, creating ever more complex patterns on the shield. In addition to the main shield of arms, various appendages came to be an integral part of the full coat of arms, or 'heraldic achievement', from the late thirteenth century onwards, such as the crest on top (derived from the decorative top-knot worn on their helmets by knights at tournaments) and in the more exalted cases supporters – beasts, birds, monsters or human figures – that stand on either side of the shield of arms and support it. In England, the use of supporters was restricted to the highest ranks of those entitled to bear arms, the Royal Family, peers and eventually the more important towns and corporations.

Arms were originally self-assumed, though famous examples of formal grants exist, such as the knighting in 1127 by Henry I of his son-in-law, Geoffrey Plantagenet, when the king hung around his neck a shield painted with golden lions. In the early fifteenth century the Crown moved against self-assumed arms. Henry V, in a series of writs, forbade the use of arms except by those entitled to them 'in right of their ancestors' or by grant from a competent authority. In the course of the fifteenth and sixteenth centuries the national regulation of arms by confirmation and grants was enforced by successive monarchs and delegated to the heralds who had formed part of the royal household since the thirteenth century, but who were constituted into a corporation, or college, by King Richard III in 1484 and given permanent premises from where to carry out their business. (Their present accommodation on the site of Derby House in the City of London has been occupied by the heralds since a grant of Queen Mary in 1555.)

Thus a system of symbolic identification which orginally related to medieval knights prospered and developed in England from the late Middle Ages onwards because the Kings of the House of Lancaster recognized social change and permitted the Kings of Arms to grant new arms to 'eminent men', and to towns, guilds, colleges and corporations. The Tudors developed the Lancastrian system further by instituting the 'Visitations' with powers of enforcement, whereby the heralds travelled the country 'policing' the use of arms, and by not restricting grants of new arms despite complaints that the then Garter King of Arms was granting armorial bearings to 'vile persons'. By these means, Henry VIII adapted heraldry to mark both status and continuing social change, and this prevented heraldry from becoming fossilized in England, as happened in France and some of the other European countries. English heraldry has continued to adapt and flourish over the centuries, with new grants of arms to the City merchants and rich lawyers who founded the new gentry families of the sixteenth and seventeenth centuries, to the soldiers, sailors, trading companies and colonial administrators who built up the British Empire in the seventeenth, eighteenth and nineteenth centuries, and to the beneficiaries of the industrial revolution, corporate as well as individual, from the eighteenth to the twentieth centuries. Thus, the towns and cities that expanded in the late Georgian and Victorian periods were granted arms just like those of the medieval boroughs: Liverpool in 1797, Manchester in 1842, Burnley in 1862 ... And naturally, the bearers of such arms proudly displayed them wherever they were able to do so. Heraldic decoration thus became a major feature of the great civic buildings of the nineteenth century.

From the later eighteenth century onwards, there was a great revival of heraldry and heraldic architectural display in general, and this went hand-in-hand with the Gothic Revival, the rise of the serious study of medieval history, and an increased pride in the antiquity and continuity of English institutions at a time when Continental Europe was being swept by French revolutionary fever. Horace Walpole, in his famous Gothick villa at Strawberry Hill, Twickenham, was one of the pioneer revivers of heraldic architectural decoration in the mid-eighteenth century as well as of Gothic in general, and he set a fashion. Wherever mock battlements or traceried windows or pinnacled skylines raised themselves so also could be expected a proud display of, often bogus, heraldry. William Beckford's Fonthill Abbey, for instance, was bedecked with all the heraldry he could command or imagine in plaster, stone and stained glass. The early nineteenth century saw the enthusiasm for the Middle Ages manifested in such projects as the grandiose reconstruction of Windsor Castle, combined with a more scholarly approach in the work of designers like Thomas Willement, 'Heraldic Artist to His Majesty King George IV'. He was responsible for reviving medieval-style heraldic painted decoration and stained glass, a revival perfected by A. W. N. Pugin who, just as he introduced a note of high seriousness into the Gothic Revival, so also helped to instil a scholarly note into architectural armorial decoration. Pugin's heraldic display on the Houses of Parliament is exemplary, and would have won the approval of Henry III himself. It set the standard for much of the Victorian revival of architectural heraldic decoration which soon outdid even the fourteenth century in scale and prolixity. To Pugin, for instance, goes the credit for reviving the heraldic encaustic tile as well as brasses and enamelwork. Nearly the whole exterior of the Houses of Parliament is encrusted with heraldry, taking its cue from the decoration of Henry VII's chapel nearby, to such a degree that the Beaufort portcullis, the heraldic device of Henry VII's mother, Lady Margaret Beaufort, has come to stand as the emblem of the Palace of Westminster itself, and of both Houses of Parliament, even being embossed on upholstery and teacups.

As the first major Victorian public building, the Houses of Parliament was a model which provided a source of inspiration for many of the splendid civic buildings of the industrial towns and cities of northern England; the great town halls, railway stations, libraries, art galleries, hospitals and law-courts of which, all made a prominent display of their newly granted coats of arms as well as other heraldic themes. At Manchester, for instance, Waterhouse's magnificent town hall is embellished not just with the arms of Manchester Corporation, but also with those of the city's trading partners in the late nineteenth century, foreign countries and other British towns and cities. The town hall at Barrow-in-Furness, also in Lancashire, has one of the most

CARDIFF, WALES, BUTE DOCK OFFICE Proudly symbolising the 'triumph of enlightened paternalism', this was designed in 1896 by William Frame in the Burges manner for the 3rd Marquess of Bute (who owned the docks) and built of red brick and terracotta. It is appropriately decorated with finely moulded shields of the Crichton-Stuart and Cardiff arms, terracotta being a material that lends itself to modelling the intricacies of heraldic design.

extensive schemes of Victorian municipal heraldry in its stained glass windows to be found anywhere. The heyday of municipal, local government and civic pride was the late nineteenth and early twentieth centuries, when the municipal corporations vied with each other in making urban improvements and erecting ambitious new buildings with their arms displayed in carved stone, embossed bronze or cast and wrought iron as tokens of honour and authority. Lamp posts, bollards, park gates, tram shelters, all were considered suitable vehicles for civic heraldry. Nor was this fashion confined to the newly armigerous boroughs and councils. The Corporation of the City of London made as proud a display of its medieval arms – *Argent a cross Gules and in the first quarter a sword erect point upwards also Gules* – in the nineteenth century, as did Manchester or Birmingham of their Victorian ones. At every major entry into the City of London the boundary is marked in the road by a short column, topped off with an heraldic dragon supporting the City arms. The various markets owned and rebuilt by the City Corporation are likewise embellished repeatedly with the dragon supporters and dragon's wing crest, as well as the shield charged with the red cross of St. George (the arms of England) and the sword of St. Paul, emblem of the City's patron saint. The City arms are typical of many of the medieval boroughs' in using emblems derived from the national arms, in their case, the red cross of St. George. York,

LONDON, CITY BOUNDARY POST ON THE EMBANKMENT All the main entrances to the City of London are marked with boundary posts with the dragon supporters and shields of the corporation's arms. Perhaps the best of them are the pair on the Victoria Embankment, just outside the Temple. These are of iron, cast by Dewar and are dated 1849. They were originally on the façade of the Coal Exchange and were moved by the City Corporation to their present site when that was demolished.

Chester, Stamford, Hereford, Faversham, the Cinq Ports and Appleby all use arms based on the ancient Royal Arms *Gules three Lions passant guardant Or*, as can be seen on their public buildings such as the Mansion House and the Bars (or gates) in the City walls at York. Today well over 500 local authorities in England and Wales bear arms by right, of which ninety date from before 1700, while the large majority have been granted in the last hundred years.

Since the Royal Arms are the most frequently displayed form of heraldry in Britain, adorning, in various historic variations as well as their contemporary form, innumerable public buildings and churches throughout the land, a few words should perhaps be said about them here. They tend to be taken for granted, yet they are of the greatest historical interest and their design reflects the many stages in the evolution of the British monarchy, as well as changes in the development of heraldic practice and design from the earliest centuries to the present day.

The Royal Arms as used today quarter the three Kingdoms of England, Scotland and Ireland. Of these, the arms of the Kingdom of England, *Gules three Lions passant guardant Or*, are the most ancient, and date back to the reign of King Richard I in the late twelfth century. Their earliest known representation is on his second Great Seal, brought into use in 1198, which shows the King on horseback holding a shield of these arms. He was the first English king to use the three lions, though from the thirteenth century these arms were 'backdated', and sometimes attributed to all the English kings from William the Conqueror onwards. The fashion for inventing legendary arms for great figures of the past who lived before heraldry was invented was a popular pastime in the later Middle Ages throughout Europe, and is seen in an extreme form in the arms attributed to Christ, the Virgin Mary and the Apostles or even Adam. The arms of Edward the Confessor, *Azure, a cross flory between five martlets Or*, which were much used by Henry III in his building works at Westminster in the mid-thirteenth century, and which can be seen, for instance, all over Westminster Abbey, are an example of such legendary posthumous

left NORWICH, NORFOLK The city arms carved on the City Hall designed by C. H. James and S. R. Pierce in 1932. Like many of the ancient borough and city arms, those of Norwich contain an allusion to the royal arms in the *lion passant guardant Or* at the bottom of the shield. The use of a stylized fortification is a feature of medieval town arms throughout Europe. The supporters (in this case angels) are a special privilege, restricted in England to the most distinguished corporations and the highest ranks of society. They first appear on the city's seal in the fifteenth century. The use of a civic fur hat rather than a crest is a feature occasionally found in old borough arms.

right STRATFORD-ON-AVON, WARWICKSHIRE Arms of the District Council over the entrance to the Council Offices in Elizabeth Street. Moulded in fibreglass by Alec Peever, a sculptor who specialises in carving good lettering and moulding heraldic decoration. These are modern arms granted to the local authority following the reorganization of local government in 1974. All but two of the new district authorities created then have applied for and received armorial bearings, continuing a tradition of civic heraldry which goes back to the adoption of seals by English boroughs in the late twelfth century. In the case of Stratford District the symbolism of the arms relates to the River Avon, the principal geographical feature of the area.

arms. It seems likely that the use of arms by the Kings of England goes back no further than Henry II, the father of Richard I. There is literary evidence (though no surviving physical evidence) that Henry II bore *Gules a Lion rampant Or*. Richard Coeur de Lion's first Great Seal had a single lion rampant, which substantiates the claim that these were the arms borne by his father. The seal of Richard's younger brother John as Lord of Ireland and Count of Mortain, struck in 1177, had a shield with two lions *passant guardant*, and it is possible that the arms with three lions on the second seal of Richard I was derived from that. It was believed by the seventeenth-century heralds such as Elias Ashmole that the third lion was added to represent Aquitaine (Richard being the immediate heir to the Dukedom of Aquitaine through his mother Eleanor), the other two lions representing England and Normandy. This, like many heraldic explanations, should be treated with a certain degree of caution.

The arms of the Kings of England retained the form assumed by Richard Coeur de Lion down to 1340, when Edward III quartered the arms of France (ancient), *Azure semy of Fleurs de lis Or*, as part of his claim to the French throne, a claim which caused the outbreak of the Hundred Years War. At some time in the first decade of the fifteenth century (the exact date is not clear), the French quartering in the Royal Arms was altered to France (modern), *Azure three Fleurs de lis Or*, in order to bring it into line with current French practice. The new arms of France quartered with England appear on Henry IV's second Great Seal which came into use during November 1406, though it is possible that the change had occurred a year or so before that.

Apart from the reign of Queen Mary in the mid-sixteenth century, when the arms of England were sometimes shown impaled with those of her husband King Philip II of Spain on seals and coins, France modern quartered with England remained the Royal Arms down to 1603 and the accession of James I, an event which led to further modifications in order to incorporate the arms of Scotland. At that time, the quartered arms of England and France were placed in the first and fourth quarters, the arms of Scotland, *Or a Lion rampant within a double Tressure flory counterflory Gules*, were placed in the second quarter, and the arms of Ireland, *Azure a Harp Or stringed Argent*, were introduced into the third quarter for the first time. The arms of Ireland were, therefore, not introduced into the Royal Achievement until the reign of James I, so as to balance Scotland, despite the fact that the Kings of England had been Lords of Ireland since the reign of John, and hereditary Kings of Ireland since the assumption of that title by Henry VIII in 1541.

During the Commonwealth, the Royal Arms, along with other trappings of monarchy, were abolished, but apart from this interruption, the Royal Arms remained the same from 1603 till the flight from the throne of James II in 1688.

After the departure of James II, the Royal Arms changed several times during the reign of his daughter Mary and her first cousin and husband William of Orange. William and Mary were proclaimed King and Queen in February 1689, and, until the Scottish Parliament recognized them in April 1689, they bore a Grand Quarter in one and four of *Quarterly France modern and England* with Ireland in two and three and an escutcheon overall for Nassau, namely *Azure billetty and a Lion rampant Or.* In April 1689, a coat was briefly adopted and appears on some coinage of (1) England, (2) Scotland, (3) Ireland, (4) France, with an escutcheon of Nassau overall. This disregarded the impartible aspect of England and France and lasted only a few months. Thereafter the arms as used by the first four Stuart sovereigns of England were re-adopted, namely (1 and 4) a Grand Quarter of France modern and England, (2) Scotland, (3) Ireland, with Nassau over all. This coat could also be impaled with a similar one omitting the escutcheon of Nassau over all to signify joint monarchs till the death of Mary, aged 32, in 1694. On the death of William and the accession of Mary's sister Anne in 1702, the escutcheon over all for Nassau was dropped, and Queen Anne bore till 1707 the traditional Stuart Royal Arms as borne by her father, uncle, grandfather and great-grandfather. The Act of Union of 1707 was signified by an impaled coat of England and Scotland in the first and fourth quarters, with France modern in the second quarter, and Ireland in the third.

On the accession of George I in 1714, the first three quarters remained the same. The fourth, which had been identical to the first, was replaced by three coats tierced per pale and per chevron for Hanover comprising (1) *Gules two Lions passant guardant Or* for Brunswick, (2) *Or semy of hearts Gules a Lion rampant Azure* for Luneburg, and (3) *Gules a Horse courant Argent* for Westphalia, with over all *an Escutcheon Gules charged with the Crown of Charlemagne Or* for the Arch-Treasurership of the Holy Roman Empire. This fourth quarter has also been blazoned as Brunswick impaling Luneburg with Westphalia, also known as Saxony ancient *entre en pointe and in an escutcheon sur tout Gules the Crown of Charlemagne Or.* There was no further change in the Royal Arms till 1801 when the French arms finally disappeared in compliance with one of the articles of the Treaty of Paris, George III also renouncing his title of King of France. At that time the arms of England were placed in the first and fourth quarters, Scotland in the second, and Ireland in the third, with the arms of Hanover (as above) placed on an escutcheon over all surmounted by the Electoral Bonnet. In 1816, Hanover became a kingdom and the Bonnet was replaced by a Royal Crown. This form of the Royal Arms survived until the accession of Queen Victoria in 1837. As a woman she was unable to succeed to the Throne of Hanover (governed in these matters by the Salic Law which enforced a strict male succession, to which the Throne of England of course was not subject) and the Hanoverian escutcheon and crown were consequently removed. Since 1837, the Royal Arms of England have remained unaltered in the form that is now generally known. As well as changes to the shield itself, the supporters of the Royal Arms have also undergone variations. The medieval Kings used supporters in a purely decorative manner and changed them frequently. Permanent royal supporters were an innovation of the Tudors and Stuarts. The first English king to use supporters is generally considered to be Edward III, who came to the throne in 1327. He is shown with dexter *a Lion guardant with a small imperial crown Or* sinister *a Hawk proper belled*

Or. His grandson and successor Richard II is said to have used the same dexter supporter and sinister *a Hart Argent attired Or*. On the other hand the privy seal of Richard II shows *two lions couchant guardant each holding an ostrich Feather charged with a scroll* as supporters. Henry IV was thought to have used dexter *an heraldic Antelope Argent ducally gorged chained maned and armed Or* and sinister *a Swan Argent similarly gorged and chained Or*.

Henry VI is given a similar dexter supporter to his grandfather Henry IV, that is *an heraldic Antelope Argent ducally gorged chained maned and armed Or* with sinister *a Leopard Argent spotted with various colours and issuing from his mouth and ears flames of fire proper* but, both at Eton College which he founded and in St. George's Chapel, Windsor, they are shown as *two heraldic Antelopes Argent armed and tufted Or*. Edward IV changed his supporters several times. They appear as dexter *a Bull Sable crowned horned unguled and membered Or* sinister *a Lion guardant Argent*, and, as the same combination reversed, *two Lions guardant Argent* and dexter *a Lion guardant Argent* sinister *a Hart Argent*. Richard II used both dexter *a Lion guardant Argent imperially crowned Or* sinister *a Boar Argent armed and bristled Or* and *two Boars Argent armed and bristled Or*. Henry VII's dexter supporter was *a Dragon Gules* and the sinister supporter was *a Greyhound Argent collared Gules*. His eldest son Prince Arthur's arms are supported on his tomb by *two heraldic Antelopes*. Initially, Henry VIII bore the same supporters as his father but later changed to dexter *a Lion guardant and imperially crowned Or* sinister *A Dragon Gules*. Edward VI and Queen Mary and Elizabeth I used the same supporters. James I retained the dexter supporter but replaced the dragon with one of the two unicorns used by him as King of Scotland and blazoned *a Unicorn Argent armed tufted and maned Or gorged with a coronet composed of crosses pattee and fleurs de lis thereto a chain affixed also Or*. These supporters have been retained to the present day.

Apart from royal and civic heraldry, the arms most likely to be met with in English towns, cities and villages are those of the local great

GLOSSOP, DERBYSHIRE The lion crest of the Howard family stands proudly over the entrance to the railway station built in 1847 by the 13th Duke of Norfolk as part of his development of Glossop as a model industrial town. This is typical of the prominent use made of the family heraldry in the great nineteenth-century aristocratic urban developments, both in London and provincial towns.

families, past and present. Thus, the arms of the Duke of Norfolk are prominent in Arundel, but also in Sheffield, Glossop and the Strand in London where he owns, or owned, property; the Duke of Northumberland's arms are prevalent at Alnwick and many other places in Northumberland which formed part of his estates. The arms of the Duke of Bedford remain a feature of the Covent Garden area of London, though the Duke's property there was sold in 1911, as well as of Woburn, his seat in Bedfordshire. The arms of the Duke of Devonshire adorn several buildings, including the Crescent, at Buxton in Derbyshire where he is lord of the manor, as well as at Eastbourne in Sussex which he developed as a seaside resort in the nineteenth century and where he still owns substantial ground rents. Sometimes it works the other way round. The Grosvenor family own so much of Westminster that when in the nineteenth century they were created dukes, they quartered as a 'coat of augmentation' the arms of the City of

26

Westminster, *a Portcullis with Chains pendant Or; a Chief of the last thereon between, on either side the united Rose of York and Lancaster, Proper, a pallet of the first charged with a Cross Flory between five Martlets also gold,* with their own medieval arms *Azure a Garb Or.* Such family arms tell the observant onlooker a great deal about the descent and inheritance of property, the benefactors of institutions and the founders of colleges, almshouses and the like.

They also throw light on wider historical events and changing political and social attitudes. The fashion for family heraldry, especially in the nineteenth century, was not just an aspect of the Gothic Revival and new medieval historical scholarship, it was also a

ARUNDEL, SUSSEX, THE DUKE OF NORFOLK'S CRESTS AT ARUNDEL CASTLE These life-size models in Coade stone of the Howard lion and the Fitzalan horse are signed 'Coade and Sealy' and were commissioned by the 12th Duke of Norfolk to ornament the Norfolk Bridge over the River Adur at Shoreham in Sussex. This was a suspension bridge built in 1833, and the crests stood on top of the pylons at either end. When the bridge was rebuilt in 1933, the Coade stone crests were rescued and re-erected at Arundel Castle.

manifestation of the seigneurial pride of the English upper classes after the French Revolution and Waterloo. The early nineteenth century in England saw the manufacture of endless Norman pedigrees, the medievalizing of surnames and titles – de Freyn, de Ramsey, Wyatville – and the undiscriminating enjoyment of all the trappings that went with such sonorous medievalism. Thus the landowner often marked all the tied cottages on his estate with carved tablets bearing his crest or full coat of arms, or had them embossed on rainwater pipes, gateposts or other ironmongery. At Holkham in Norfolk, the iron door of every cottage oven was embossed with the ostrich crest of the Cokes. At Arundel the cast-iron bollards in the streets of the town bear the ducal lion of the Norfolks, and the suspension bridge at Shoreham, built by the 12th Duke of Norfolk, was splendidly embellished with life-size versions of his supporters standing on top of each of the pylons. Humphrey Repton in the *Red Book* for improving the park at Tatton in Cheshire advised his client there, Wilbraham Egerton, to decorate all the milestones along the public roads on the estate with the Egerton arms to impress on the passer-by the extent of his property. The heraldic inn sign, however, which became widespread in this period, continues to be a common feature. Nearly every village and every town has at least one pub displaying the arms of a past or present local family. They even continue to be augmented. In 1955, the 'Green Dragon' at Downham in Lancashire, for instance, changed its name to the 'Assheton Arms' on the elevation of the local squire, Sir Ralph Assheton, to the peerage as the 1st Lord Clitheroe, and its façade was suitably embellished with a large heraldic signboard to match. More recently, the pub at Hainton in Lincolnshire changed its name from the 'Hainton Inn' to the 'Heneage Arms' and now sports the appropriate heraldry.

ALNWICK, NORTHUMBERLAND The early fourteenth-century castle barbican has the Percy lion rampant *Azure* carved on a panel over the archway. The inner gatehouse, restored by Salvin, has a Victorian panel of a lion supporter holding a banner of the Northumberland arms quartering Percy and Lucy, inspired by the genuine medieval heraldic carving at Warkworth Castle.

below FRAMLINGHAM, SUFFOLK
The arms of the 2nd Duke of Norfolk over the gateway to the castle. These were carved *circa* 1513 and show the full achievement of the duke, who inherited Framlingham Castle from the Mowbrays and who was restored as 2nd Duke of Norfolk in 1513 following his great victory against the Scots at Flodden Field (the title having been attainted following the death in battle of his father on the wrong side at Bosworth). The duke was very proud of his descent from the Mowbrays and the six quarterings on this shield make the point. They comprise Howard, Brotherton (marking his royal descent from Edward I), Warren, Mowbray, Segrave and Braose of Gower. As well as the second quartering with the ancient royal arms of England, the crest too marks the royal descent of the Dukes of Norfolk, for it is the lion of the royal arms differenced with a ducal coronet round his neck and with his tail straightened.

facing page LONDON, CHARING CROSS Replica of the Eleanor Cross designed by E. M. Barry in 1863 and paid for by the railway company as an ornament to the forecourt of the railway station. The heraldic carving was the work of Thomas Earp, the leading purveyor of architectural sculpture in the Victorian period, who worked on a wide range of churches and country houses as well as public buildings, of which the Palace of Westminster is the most notable. The arms include the royal arms of Edward I and his wife Eleanor of Castile, the latter being the earliest example in English heraldry of the practice of *quartering* arms, an innovation developed in Spain and which spread from there across all Europe (except Poland).

left YORK, MONK BAR This engraving of 1807 by Halfpenny shows the gateway before the removal of the outer barbican in 1825. The shields of arms displayed under Gothic fretted canopies include two shields of the city arms with those of the Lancastrian kings above. This royal shield gives a clue to the dating of the upper part of the Bar, which is usually vaguely said to be fourteenth-century. It must, in fact, be early fifteenth-century as it incorporates the quartering of *France Modern*, only adopted by Henry IV *circa* 1406.

facing page YORK, BOOTHAM BAR The medieval gateways in the city walls of York are embellished with the arms of the King and of York itself. On Bootham Bar the topmost shield displays the *three lions passant guardant Or* of the English royal arms, while the pair of shields below have the arms of the city – *Argent on a cross Gules five lions passant guardant Or*. These national and royal emblems are appropriate to the second city of England and onetime seat of the Council of the North.

EASTGATE STREET, CHESTER This famous historic street with its half-timbered gabled houses and gateway in the medieval city walls owes much of its character to Victorian reconstruction and elaboration. The ornament on the buildings is rich in heraldry. In this photographic view, the hanging wrought-iron sign of the Grosvenor Hotel is a prominent feature with its shield of the Grosvenor arms – *Azure a garb Or*. Eastgate itself was rebuilt in 1768 and is embellished on the keystone of the archway by a typical Georgian cartouche (substituting a decorative rococo shape for the shield) bearing the city arms which date back to the Middle Ages, but were confirmed by the Heralds in 1580. The shield contains the Royal Arms of England joined to those of the old Earls of Chester by 'dimidiation', whereby half the lions are shown and one and a half wheatsheafs (or garbs). The Diamond Jubilee clock on top of the gateway was erected to the design of the Chester architect John Douglas in 1897 and is a jolly piece of wrought iron, again embellished with the city heraldry but shown on two separate shields, one the royal arms of England and one the Earls of Chester with the wheatsheafs.

top NORWICH, NORFOLK, THE
GUILDHALL, MARKET PLACE This
early sixteenth-century doorway is
embellished with three shields of arms.
In the centre are the royal arms of
Henry VIII with supporters. On the left
are the arms of the city corporation and
on the right are the Bassingham arms
recording the builder of the doorway,
which was originally on a house in
London Street and was moved to the
Guildhall later.

bottom BRISTOL, THE CATHEDRAL
PRECINCT Until the reign of Henry
VIII, Bristol Cathedral was an Augustinian Abbey (founded in 1142) and more
of the conventual buildings survive than
at any other Augustinian site in
England. The gatehouse is late Norman,
its arch carved with typical zig-zag
decoration. It was partly reconstructed
circa 1500 by Abbot Newland and the
heraldry shown here dates his work
with its twin shields of Abbot Newland's own arms and those of the Berkeley family, overlords of the surrounding
parts of Gloucestershire. Abbots and
other churchmen frequently received
grants of personal arms in the early
Tudor period, an expensive luxury as
they did not have descendants who
could inherit them.

top BRISTOL, KING STREET SEAMEN'S ALMSHOUSES OR MERCHANT VENTURERS' ALMSHOUSES founded by the Merchant Venturers of Bristol in the seventeenth century. This panel on the facade displays the arms granted to the Society in 1569, one of the supporters being a mermaid, redolent of Bristol and the society's seafaring character. Their motto, not included in this panel, is a line from the first Ode of Horace: 'In docilis pauperium pati'. The almshouses were erected in 1696 as a complete quadrangle, but one range was destroyed by bombing in the Second World War.

bottom BRISTOL, BROAD STREET, TAYLORS' HALL, TAYLORS' COURT This was formerly the Hall of the Merchant Taylors' Guild, a livery company similar to the medieval guilds of London founded in 1399. The Hall was built in 1740 and its principal feature is the door protected by the shell hood shown here, marvellously embellished with the guilds' arms. The crest, a lamb, is the symbol of St John the Baptist, patron saint of the guild, while the supporters are a pair of jolly camels *Or* with prominent humps.

below PENRITH, CUMBERLAND The Gloucester Arms public house displays a particularly fine heraldic inn sign, a sixteenth-century carved panel of the arms of King Richard III, formerly Duke of Gloucester. Richard III was born at Middleham Castle in Yorkshire and spent much time in the north of England, where his arms and wild boar badge and supporters are still frequently encountered.

above ASHBY-DE-LA-ZOUCHE, LEICESTERSHIRE The Bull's Head Inn in Market Street. This photograph, taken in 1874, shows the Tudor parget-ted decoration on the gable with the arms of Henry VIII encircled by the Garter and supported by the lion and dragon. It is possible to differentiate between the medieval and early Tudor royal arms because of changes in the supporters. Henry VIII introduced the dragon which survived till it was displaced by the unicorn from the Scottish royal arms when James I ascended the English throne.

ST JOHN'S COLLEGE, CAMBRIDGE
The front of the gatehouse is a charac-
teristic late-medieval display of heraldic
carving, gorgeously repainted in the
correct colours by Professor Tristram,
the expert on medieval murals. The
college was founded in 1511 by Lady
Margaret Beaufort, Countess of Rich-
mond and Derby, the mother of Henry
VII, and the arms are hers. The shield
has the royal arms differenced with a
bordure of *Argent* and *Azure* (the
Lancastrian colours) recording her
descent from John of Gaunt. The supporters are *two yales Argent bezanty,
armed, unguled and tufted Or*. Such
mythical beasts are typical of late medi-

eval armory, the repertory of which was
enlarged by a whole range of fabulous
monsters invented by the heralds. Yales
have antelopes' bodies, goats' heads and
elephants' tails. The main achievement
is flanked by two badges, the Beaufort
portcullis and the red rose of Lancaster,
the latter surmounted by a royal crown
in allusion to the accession to the throne
of her son, Henry VII. Her own coronet, as it appears above the portcullis
badge and the shield of arms, is made
up of marguerites, and the same flowers
are carved all over the background, a
charming pun on the Christian name of
the foundress.

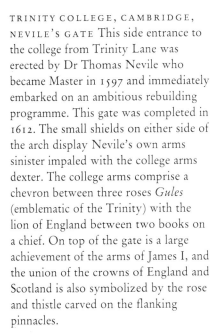

TRINITY COLLEGE, CAMBRIDGE, NEVILE'S GATE This side entrance to the college from Trinity Lane was erected by Dr Thomas Nevile who became Master in 1597 and immediately embarked on an ambitious rebuilding programme. This gate was completed in 1612. The small shields on either side of the arch display Nevile's own arms sinister impaled with the college arms dexter. The college arms comprise a chevron between three roses *Gules* (emblematic of the Trinity) with the lion of England between two books on a chief. On top of the gate is a large achievement of the arms of James I, and the union of the crowns of England and Scotland is also symbolized by the rose and thistle carved on the flanking pinnacles.

QUEEN'S COLLEGE, CAMBRIDGE, SHIELD OF ARMS IN THE FIRST COURT The arms are those granted the college in 1575 and this carving records that grant as it was set up that year over the entrance to the fifteenth-century hall. They are based on those of the co-founders of the college, Margaret of Anjou, wife of King Henry VI and daughter of René, Duke of Anjou. The six quarterings represent the Anjou family's dignities, lordships and claims, namely: Hungary, Anjou (Ancient), Jerusalem, Anjou (Modern), Bar and Lorraine. The crest is an eagle. The arms were carved by Thomas Gray and make a neat piece of Elizabethan classical design.

39

CAMBRIDGE, HOBSON'S CONDUIT IN TRUMPINGTON STREET This originally stood in Market Hill but was moved as an obstruction to traffic. It was built in 1614 at the Cambridge end of the 'new river' made to bring fresh water from Nine Wells near Trumpington to Cambridge. The hexagonal structure is crowned with an ogee cupola and fanciful ornament of strapwork and heraldry with the royal arms of James I. This type of street ornament is a reminder of the more temporary wooden decorations embellished with heraldry that were frequently erected in the Elizabethan and Jacobean periods to mark important events.

40

NUNEHAM COURTENAY, OXFORD-
SHIRE CARFAX CONDUIT This was
moved from Carfax in Oxford, where it
was in the way of traffic, and re-erected
by Lord Harcourt at Nuneham Courtenay in 1787. It was originally built in
the sixteenth century as a street ornament, a fabulous Elizabethan recreation
of a market cross, bristling with heraldic
beasts holding small banners. It is a rare
survival of a type of three-dimensional
heraldic ornament which was once
common in English towns. Perhaps one
day it will be taken back to Oxford?

ORIEL COLLEGE, OXFORD Eighteenth-century cartouche of arms in the Back Quad, a typical early eighteenth-century way of displaying heraldry in a scrolling framework with ambiguous carved masks at top and bottom. By transmuting the shield into an abstract Baroque shape, coats of arms were transformed into architectural ornaments suitable for use in pediments, and gables, or over doors and windows.

ORIEL COLLEGE, OXFORD The early seventeenth-century main gates (circa 1640) are carved with (from left to right) the arms of the college, the Stuart Royal Arms (this part of the college was rebuilt in the reign of Charles I), the Prince of Wales feathers (the titular founder, Edward II, was first Prince of Wales) and the arms of John Tolson, provost of the college at the time that the Front Quad was rebuilt between 1620 and 1642. This is a fine and well-preserved example of early seventeenth-century heraldic decoration in carved wood.

CHRIST CHURCH, OXFORD The vault over the gateway from St Aldate's to Tom Quad is studded with shields of arms. In pride of place round the central wreath are, at the top, the arms of Henry VIII and at the bottom those of Cardinal Wolsey, the founder, and of the college itself, and at the sides Charles II and the Duke of York (later James II). The smaller shields at the top of the fans include those of many famous English families: Howard, Seymour, Spencer, Cavendish, Herbert, Berkeley, Stanley and Russell among others. The fan vault was designed by Christopher Wren who completed Wolsey's gatehouse (left incomplete in 1529 at the time of his fall from power) in 1681–2 and deliberately kept to the Gothic style for, as he wrote to Dr Fell, the Dean of Christ Church in 1681, 'I resolved it ought to be Gothic to agree with the Founder's work.' The display of heraldry is one of the details of the design which enables the seventeenth-century Gothic Revival work to be differentiated from the late-Perpendicular original.

43

top ALL SOULS, OXFORD Wrought iron gates of splendid Baroque design in Nicholas Hawksmoor's Baroque Gothic North Quad (1734). The overthrow incorporates the college arms which are the personal coat of the founder (1438) Henry Chichele, Archbishop of Canterbury. The display of arms in the overthrow of wrought iron gates was one of the most attractive heraldic decorative innovations of the seventeenth- and eighteenth-century blacksmiths.

bottom MAGDALEN COLLEGE, OXFORD The High Street gateway is embellished with shields of the Lancastrian royal arms (Henry VI was king when the college was founded in 1458) and the college arms which are those of its founder, Bishop Waynflete, Bishop of Winchester. As medieval clergy had no legitimate descendants, their arms are often used without differencing. The shields with W. monograms are not strictly heraldic, but also commemorate the college's founder, while its dedication to the Blessed Virgin Mary is marked by the Ms on the label stops. This gateway designed by Bodley and Garner in 1885 is an example of the Victorian Gothic Revival at its most sumptuous. The alternation of shields and badges in the form of roses of Lancaster is perfectly integrated into the design of the crenellated parapet. Waynflete's arms comprised his family shield – *Lozengy Ermine and Sable* – to which he added a *chief Sable with three lilies slipped Argent* borrowed from the shield of Eton College, marking the fact that he was its Provost.

ETON, BUCKINGHAMSHIRE
Wrought-iron gates with the arms of
the college. The shield is designed to
appear as if hung from a *trompe* iron
strap. The arms, dating from 1443,
comprise *Sable three lily flowers Argent*,
commemorating the dedication of the
college to St Mary at Eton, *a chief per
pale azure and gules charged on the
dexter side with a fleur de lis and on the
sinister with a lion passant guardant Or*,
recalling the royal founder, Henry VI,
who was King of England and of
France.

LONDON, THE CHARTERHOUSE,
CHARTERHOUSE SQUARE This rare
surviving example of a Tudor nobleman's town palace occupies the site of
the medieval charterhouse, secularized
by Henry VIII. It was substantially
reconstructed by the 4th Duke of Norfolk in the years leading up to his ex-
ecution on a trumped-up charge of
treason in 1572. The full achievement of
the duke's arms with supporters and
crests is carved in three dimensions over
the porch leading into the great hall.
Later, the Charterhouse was acquired
by Thomas Sutton and given by him to
the school which still bears the name,
though it moved to Surrey in the nineteenth century. His arms appear on the
painted sundial in the middle of the
great hall parapet.

facing page NEWBURY, BERKSHIRE, RAYMOND'S ALMSHOUSES IN ARGYLE ROAD Old charitable benefactions often display, as here, the arms of their founder, and thereby record his generosity for posterity. The picturesque Tudor appearance of this building is largely due to a restoration of 1927–8. The building is thought to have begun life as farm buildings, but was converted into a house in the sixteenth century and became Raymond's Almshouses in 1676.

above NORWICH, THE DEANERY Tudor coat of arms over the main entrance. The possessors of certain offices, including senior clergy, the Regius Professors and heads of colleges at Oxford and Cambridge, and the Kings of Arms are entitled to impale the arms of their office. Here the dean's personal arms are impaled with those of Norwich Cathedral.

top left LONDON, COVENT GARDEN PIAZZA The Market Building visible through the arch on the right has the Russell arms with a ducal coronet in the central pediment, commemorating John Russell, 6th Duke of Bedford, who built it in 1828–30. Originally the kitchen garden of Westminster Abbey, Covent Garden passed to the Russells after the dissolution of the monasteries in the reign of Henry VIII and was developed by them between the seventeenth and nineteenth centuries, their arms appearing on many buildings and gateways in the area.

above LONDON, ST. MARTIN-IN-THE-FIELDS Royal arms in the pediment designed by James Gibbs: a splendid example of the discriminating use of heraldry by leading eighteenth-century architects who adapted it to the constraints of classical forms, here the triangular proportions of the pediment.

top right LONDON, COVENT GARDEN Gateway to St Paul's churchyard, with the Bedford arms in the overthrow. The church was built to the design of Inigo Jones by the Earl of Bedford at this own expense in 1638; the arms commemorate his generosity.

HIGH WYCOMBE, BUCKINGHAM-
SHIRE, THE GUILDHALL Designed
by Henry Keene in 1757 and splendidly
sited as a view-stopper at the west end
of the High Street, this handsome
public building was the gift to the town
of John, the 1st Earl of Shelburne, and
his generosity is recorded for posterity
by the display of his personal arms in
the pediment rather than those of the
borough of High Wycombe which
would have been more usual in this
situation.

ALNWICK, NORTHUMBERLAND
Bridge over the River, Alne, designed
by John Adam in 1773 for the 1st Duke
of Northumberland and proudly embellished with the Northumberland crest, a
lion with a straight tail, cast in lead. The
arms of the Percys, Earls and Dukes of
Northumberland, are prominent
throughout the county of
Northumberland.

INVERBRORA, SUTHERLAND House
built in 1821 as part of the improvement
of the Dunrobin Castle estate by
George Granville Leveson-Gower, 2nd
Marquess of Stafford (later 1st Duke of
Sutherland) and his wife Elizabeth, an
heiress who was Countess of Sutherland
in her own right. The twin heraldic
tablet over the front door sports both
their arms with the appropriate coronets
of rank. This is typical of nineteenth-
century model estate buildings which
are often embellished with the crest or
the full arms of the landowner.

WOBURN, BEDFORDSHIRE The porch of the old school designed by William Blore in the Tudor-Revival style for the 6th Duke of Bedford in the mid-nineteenth century, with his arms carved on a tablet over the entrance. Such an heraldic tablet is a common feature of nineteenth-century model estate buildings, and here it celebrates the Duke's philanthropy in rebuilding the school at his own expense.

WOBURN, BEDFORDSHIRE The London Lodge to Woburn Abbey on the south side of the town. Woburn, like several small towns in the shadow of the principal seat of a great nobleman, has many heraldic allusions to the source of its well-being, in this case the Duke of Bedford. Designed by Henry Holland in 1790, the heraldry over the archway is a nice compromise between strict armorial accuracy and classical design. The goat crest is detached from the rest of the achievement and placed in a panel like an antique sculpted relief.

LONDON, GROSVENOR OFFICE, 53
DAVIES STREET The Grosvenor family
crest and coronet, modelled in stucco,
embellish the flanking panels on the
parapet of the facade designed by
Thomas Cundy II (the estate surveyor)
in 1836. The Grosvenor family developed and still own all the surrounding part of Mayfair.

left SHEFFIELD, YORKSHIRE Temporary arch erected for a visit of the Prince of Wales (later Edward VII) to Sheffield in 1875. This jolly piece of medieval make-believe was designed by M. E. Hadfield, the Sheffield architect, for the 15th Duke of Norfolk, who was the largest landowner in Sheffield, his family having inherited the estates there of the Talbots, Earls of Shrewsbury, in the seventeenth century. The painted heraldry on the arch records the descent of the lordship of Hallam from the Furnivals, and through the Talbots to the Howards, with the arms of the duke himself in the centre over the archway.

facing page SOUTHPORT, LANCASHIRE Gazebo in the grounds of Meols Hall, designed by its owner Roger Hesketh in 1963 and sporting his arms on a shield over the entrance, a good example of the continuity of traditional heraldry on the landed estate.

left CITY OF LONDON, THE GUILD-
HALL, showing a detail of George
Dance's Saracenic Gothick frontispiece
of 1788–9. The arms of the City Corporation supported by a pair of splendidly fierce dragons crown the parapet.
The motto 'Domine Dirige Nos' (Lord
Direct Us) is carved on the frieze panel
below, making this an exceptionally
well-integrated piece of heraldic architecture. The shield combines the cross
of St George (the arms of England) with
the emblem of the City's patron, St Paul
(the sword having been the instrument
of his martyrdom), This shield of arms

was already in use in the thirteenth
century while the dragon supporters
were added in the seventeenth century,
making the arms of the City Corporation among the most venerable
examples of English civic arms.

right CITY OF LONDON The City
Corporation's arms cut out of the
wrought-iron weathervane on top of the
Guildhall. The sword of St Paul, as well
as appearing in its correct position in
the first quarter of the shield, also forms
the top-most finial.

top CITY OF LONDON Smithfield Market, rebuilt to the design of Sir Horace Jones in 1866–7. The arms of the City Corporation occupy a painted roundel in the central gable while the dragon supporters in cast iron fill the spandrels above the arch, an excellent example of the imaginative integration of heraldry into the design of a building, as well as being a bravura use of the material.

bottom CITY OF LONDON Lamp-post on Holborn Viaduct decorated with the dragon supporters of the arms of the City corporation. Designed in 1863–9 by the corporation surveyor, William Heywood (with the assistance of Thomas Blashill in the detailing), the Holborn Viaduct is typical of many nineteenth-century civic works in making good decorative use of the corporation's heraldry, as well as exploiting the possibilities of cast iron as an ornamental building material.

LONDON, THE GOLDSMITHS' HALL
The twelve great livery companies of the City of London were among the first organizations to receive corporate arms, and they are also among the organizations with the proud privilege of having supporters. The beautiful carving on the front of the Goldsmiths' Hall, designed by Philip Hardwick in 1829–35, shows their full achievement with shield, helmet and crest, supporters and motto. It was the work of S. Nixon, who was responsible for all the decorative carving on the building. The Goldsmiths' Company is among the richest and oldest of the City Fraternities, a guild of goldsmiths being recorded as early as 1180. The shield is borne by prescriptive right and is recorded in the fifteenth century, while the crest and supporters were added by formal grant in 1571. The charges on the shield symbolize the union of the delegated royal privilege of assay (of which the leopard's head is the emblem) with the trade of goldsmith (represented by the cup and buckles). The demi-virgin of the crest is an allusion to Elizabeth I in whose reign the grant of a crest was made.

LONDON, THE GOLDSMITHS' HALL
The rich cast-iron gates at the entrance
display shields of arms of the City
Corporation and of the Goldsmiths'
Company. The leopard's head which
appears in the first and fourth quarters
of the latter, appears again in the centre
of the doorhead in a marvellously ex-
pressive piece of stone carving by
Nixon. The leopard's head of the Goldsmiths' arms is well known as it appears
among the assay marks with which they
stamp all English gold and silver work.
In 1300, an Act of Edward I's laid down
that all 'arts of gold and silver' should
be assayed by the Wardens of the Goldsmiths' Company and stamped with the
leopard's head to testify the quality of
the metals, and this ancient privilege has
survived down to the present day.

top PRESTON, LANCASHIRE, THE CORN EXCHANGE in Lune Street was erected by the town corporation in 1832, with their arms carved on the pediment. The arms of Preston probably date back to the sixteenth century for, despite its largely nineteenth-century industrial character, the town is an ancient borough and received its first charter in 1179. The PP below the lamb stands for Preston; the incorporation of letters in the arms is a very unusual feature in English heraldry (though not of Spanish). The Holy Lamb is the emblem of St. John the Baptist to whom the ancient parish church was re-dedicated when it was rebuilt in the sixteenth century. The arms are recorded as being already in use in the early seventeenth-century heraldic visitations of Lancashire. The somewhat florid shape of the shield is typical of Georgian heraldic design.

bottom READING, BERKSHIRE, ROYAL BERKSHIRE HOSPITAL, LONDON ROAD Designed by Henry Briant and built in 1837–9, it is an exceptionally splendid hospital in the Greek Revival style. The giant Ionic portico contains the royal arms in the pediment proclaiming the county's proud soubriquet of the 'Royal County of Berkshire', thanks to the sovereign's proximity at Windsor Castle. A full achievement of arms with supporters is ideally suited to the triangular proportion of a pediment and was much used by classical architects for that reason.

LONDON, BURLINGTON ARCADE
The Chesham arms over the North
entrance. The Burlington Arcade was
developed on a narrow patch of ground
alongside Burlington House in 1815–19
by the Cavendish family. It later de-
scended to a cadet branch of the family
created Lords Chesham, and it is their
arms which are placed on the facades of
the Arcade in Piccadilly and Burlington
Gardens. The latter, shown in this
photograph, was remodelled to the
design of Beresford Pite in 1930.

LONDON, PENHALIGON'S,
WELLINGTON STREET, COVENT
GARDEN A recent revival of the Georgian shop front with dark painted join-
ery and with the Prince of Wales's
warrant displayed over the doorway.
Since 1907 the display of royal warrants
on shop fronts has been restricted to the
Sovereign, Sovereign's consort and the
heir to the throne.

BY APPOINTMENT TO
HER MAJESTY THE QUEEN
SILVERSMITHS
MAPPIN & WEBB LTD LONDON

LONDON, MAPPIN AND WEBB, REGENT STREET Royal Warrant carved on slate by Alec Peever, a good example of a modern royal warrant which owes its inspiration to the engravings of the late Reynolds Stone. There is no enforced version of the royal arms for use in the display on shop fronts of royal warrants and this gives scope for individual traders to commission good contemporary designs and craftsmanship if they so wish, though the Royal Warrant Holders' Association, a professional body, has to approve the design and keeps a list of recommended firms for producing versions of the royal arms for this purpose.

above LONDON, HENRY VII'S CHAPEL, WESTMINSTER Late medieval heraldic display on both secular and religious buildings reached its ultimate prominence in the reign of Henry VII, when the heraldry of the new Tudor dynasty was lavishly carved all over the royal building projects. Everywhere at Henry VII Chapel, the walls are enlivened by deeply undercut roses and portcullises, while little heraldic beasts support gilded heraldic banners on top of the pinnacles. Henry VII's Chapel provided the key inspiration for the even more extensive scheme of heraldic decoration devised by Pugin for the Palace of Westminster in the nineteenth century.

facing page, left LONDON, MIDDLE TEMPLE HALL The Inns of Court are rich hunting grounds for heraldry. Crests, supporters and whole achievements are to be found on porches, over gateways, included in ironwork designs or filling gables and pediments. Here the finely coloured crest of the Middle Temple, the symbol of St John, enlivens the entrance porch of Middle Temple Hall (built in 1562).

facing page, right LONDON, CHARLES I STATUE AT CHARING CROSS This bronze statue by Le Seur narrowly missed being melted down during the Commonwealth, and was set up in its present position in 1675 at which time it was given the high sculpted plinth by Joshua Marshal with the royal arms, which are now picturesquely weathered.

facing page, left CHEADLE, STAFFORDSHIRE CATHOLIC CHURCH OF ST GILES Designed by A. W. Pugin in 1841 for the 15th Earl of Shrewsbury, this is Pugin's masterpiece. The west doors are among the most startling uses of heraldry in the whole of English architecture. Each is painted *Gules* and sports a *Lion Rampant Or within a bordure engrailed Or*, the Shrewsbury arms. Pugin called St Giles 'a perfect revival of an English parish church of the time of Edward I', and that goes for the coats of arms as well as the Gothic detail.

facing page, right LONDON, THE PALACE OF WESTMINSTER The exterior is encrusted with heraldic decoration displayed in Perpendicular panels, on bosses, corbels and pinnacles, all designed by A. W. Pugin who was responsible here for making the Victorian heraldic revival as serious as the Victorian Gothic revival. He was inspired by such genuine medieval examples as the George Hotel at Glastonbury, and of course the nearby Henry VII's Chapel, which explains the prevalence of Tudor heraldic badges, including the rose of Lancaster and the Beaufort portcullis. The chief carvers employed to provide architectural sculpture for these facades were Thomas Earp and J. B. Philips.

right LONDON, COVENT GARDEN, THE FORMER WESTMINSTER FIRE OFFICE IN KING STREET The principal feature of the façade is the splendid stucco coat of arms with portcullis, and ostrich feather crest. It lends considerable distinction to the Italianate palazzo façade, remodelled by Charles Mayhew in 1857.

left ARMAGH, NORTHERN IRELAND
Bank in Upper English Street designed
by Charles Lanyion *circa* 1850 with the
arms of the city of Belfast fitted neatly
into the top of the arch over the
entrance.

facing page, left CITY OF LONDON,
TEMPLE BAR Guarding the main
processional entrance to the City of
London via Fleet Street, this Italianate
structure, designed by Sir Horace Jones
in 1880, is surmounted by the corporation's arms supported by an energetic-
looking dragon modelled by C. B.
Birch. The Italian character of the
architecture is carried through into the
heraldry in the form of the Quattro-
cento 'horse's head' shield, a shape
unique to Italian Renaissance heraldic
design and not otherwise to be encountered in England.

facing page, right LONDON, MIDDLE-
SEX GUILDHALL, PARLIAMENT
SQUARE Designed by J. S. Gibson in
Art Nouveau Gothic style in 1906, this
former headquarters of Middlesex
County Council amply demonstrates
the confidence of early twentieth-
century local government and flaunts a
prominent display of the council's arms
carved by Henry Fehr. The Middlesex
arms are based on those assigned by the
medieval heralds to the ancient kingdom
of the middle Saxons. The three swords
or seaxes are a pun on Saxon. The
county of Essex uses similar arms.

left LONDON, THE STRAND Lamp-
post with the arms of the City of Westminster, the local authority, on the base,
embossed in cast iron.

right LONDON, LAMP POST ON THE
EMBANKMENT with the arms of the
former London County Council
(granted in 1914). The blue and silver
wavy lines represent the River Thames,
while the cross of St George (the
national emblem) and the royal lion are
an appropriate reminder that London is
the capital of England. Also used by the
Greater London Council, these arms are
already an historical curiosity.

above CITY OF LONDON, QUEEN
VICTORIA STREET Mansion House
Buildings, designed by John Belcher
with the arms of the City corporation in
the gable over the entrance.

left LONDON, DEAN'S YARD, WEST-
MINSTER The arms of Westminster
School, over the entrance on west side,
with finely carved angel supporters.

71

EDINBURGH, ST ANDREW'S HOUSE, CALTON HILL Built in 1936–9 to accommodate the principal departments of the Scottish Office and designed by Thomas Tait, St Andrew's House makes impressive use of the royal arms, as used in Scotland (with the unicorn supporter to dexter and the Scottish royal lion in the first quarter), over the main entrance. The shield itself was the work of Alexander Carrick and the supporters were carved by Phyllis Bone.

LONDON, CHURCH HOUSE, WEST-MINSTER Designed in 1937 by Sir Herbert Baker as offices for the Church of England, the elevation is studded with shields of the arms of all the different Anglican bishoprics in England carved by Charles Wheeler. Baker was a great enthusiast for heraldry and made much use of it in his architecture.

above BURY ST EDMUND'S,
SUFFOLK, SUFFOLKSHIRE HALL
This mild classical survival design by
McMorran and Whitby of 1968 makes
effective use of the arms of West Suffolk
County Council to relieve the well-
proportioned expanses of plain brick-
work and to provide a counterpoint to
the regular rhythm of window open-
ings. The arms are based on the legendary arms of Edward the Confessor, on
the grounds that St Edmund, King and
Martyr, Bury's patron saint, was a
member of the same royal dynasty.

overleaf LONDON, HYDE PARK
CORNER, ROYAL ARTILLERY
MEMORIAL Erected in 1925 by the
distinguished sculptor C. S. Jagger, this
marvellously blocky, stripped classical
design is boldly embellished with a large
carving of the royal arms, which makes
a significant contribution to the overall
composition.

Long may this heraldic tradition continue. Coats of arms introduce colour, beautiful design and the shorthand of history into the often drab, damp streets of English town centres. Pub signs, royal warrants, civic pomp and family pride add immensely to the pleasure to be derived by the passer-by, whether sight-seer, shopper or worker going about his ordinary business. There are no hard and fast rules about the decorative display of heraldry. It is very much a matter of individual taste, though if it is inaccurate or badly designed, it can look ridiculous, and it is important that heraldry should be integrated into the architectural design of a building and not just stuck on any old how. It is a pity that several of the large brewing companies do not make more effort to get their pub signs properly designed and painted, or even heraldically correct. Around Masham, in Yorkshire, for example, there are several pubs named the 'Bruce Arms'. They currently depict on their signs a spider and cobweb in reference to Robert the Bruce, the Scottish patriot. This is an ignorant solecism. The pub names refer to the Brudenell-Bruce family, Marquesses of Ailesbury, who at one time owned the Jervaulx Abbey estate. These inn signs should be painted *Or a Saltire and Chief Gules, on a canton Argent a Lion rampant Azure.* Then there is the hopelessness of organizations like British Rail which has a perfectly decent coat of arms and crest, granted in 1956 by Garter and the Lord Lyon Kings of Arms to the British Transport Commission, after the railways had been nationalized by the Attlee government, but instead uses a hideous 1960s logo, like a swastika, which contributes to the generally squalid appearance of its railway stations and other property; and which has also allowed the splendid regional heraldry of the old railway companies to fall into abeyance. There is a strong argument for reviving heraldic Visitations for policing the use of coats of arms. Organizations, like British Rail, which refuse to display their proper arms, or breweries which get their pub signs wrong should be heavily fined and the proceeds used to endow scholarships to train new generations of heraldic artists to enable the ancient crafts of heraldic design, painting and carving to continue to flourish and to embellish our towns and cities.

LONDON, ST PANCRAS STATION
Detail of coats of arms on the *porte cochère*. Sir Gilbert Scott's magnificent Gothic architecture naturally makes use of heraldry, including the arms of the proud Midland Railway Company, whose showpiece this station once was, together with the industrial towns and cities served by the railway such as Derby, Leicester, Nottingham and Sheffield. What a decline from this to the sleazy visual image of contemporary British Rail.

LONDON, BLACKFRIARS RAILWAY BRIDGE Of all the many heraldic displays in cast iron on Victorian bridges, this is perhaps the most splendid example. Dated 1864, it depicts the arms of the main places served by the former London, Chatham and Dover Railway Company surmounted by a large V for Victoria and a royal crown. Reading clockwise from the top, the arms are Kent, Dover, Rochester and the City of London.

above CHESTER, THE RAILWAY STATION This photograph taken in the 1960s, shows the crest of British Rail in a central roundel – a demi-lion *rampant* holding a locomotive wheel *issuant* from an heraldic crown on which are arranged the English rose, the Scottish thistle and the Welsh leek. British Rail no longer uses either its own arms and crest or those of the old regional railway companies which it has superceded; instead it uses a logo unworthy of the fine architectural design of many of the great Victorian railway stations which it owns.

left LONDON, KING'S CROSS STATION The hideous British Rail logo contributes to the squalid appearance of the station, whereas a well-designed display of heraldry would enhance the appearance of the station. British Rail is among the worst offenders in choosing to inflict on the public a display of debased 1960s 'graphic design' rather than its own heraldry or that of the regional companies to which it is the successor.

facing page, left LONDON, YORK-SHIRE BUILDING, THE STRAND This post-war Neo-Georgian building (1958 by W. Braxton Sinclair) is the head-quarters of the Yorkshire Building Society, the arms of which are to be found on various parts of the façade. The ram's head crests over the entrance recall that the prosperity of Yorkshire was based on wool.

facing page, right LONDON, BARCLAYS BANK, 160 PICCADILLY Hanging sign with eagle arms of the bank. This splendid design is perfectly matched to the scale and character of the building, and was erected in 1985.

right LONDON, COVENT GARDEN, NATIONAL WESTMINSTER BANK, HENRIETTA STREET The hideous modern sign with its meaningless logo is a blot on the elevation of an otherwise dignified building. The National West-minster Bank has a decent coat of arms and has no excuse for inflicting this type of debased visual trash on the public. The correct arms of the bank appear in enamel on the well-designed bronze night safe, which has somehow so far escaped the new illiterate 'corporate house-style'.

LONDON, THE FINSBURY HEALTH
CENTRE Designed by Lubetkin, one of
the pioneer Modern architects working
in England, this building shows how
traditional heraldry, in this case the
arms of the former borough of Finsbury, could be satisfactorily incorporated into the design even of architecture
in the International Modern manner.
The arms were granted in 1931 and are
typical of the over-elaboration of later
municipal heraldry with references to
the Order of St John, New River, Charterhouse, Aldersgate, Clerkenwell and
other historical constituents of the
borough.

SHORT GLOSSARY OF
HERALDIC TERMS

Ancient Arms formerly borne in fact or legend.

Annulet A ring.

Argent Silver

Augmentation An additional charge, usually a mark of honour.

Azure Blue.

Badge A free-standing heraldic device.

Bar Horizontal stripe.

Base Lower part of shield.

Bend Diagonal stripe.

Bezant Gold roundel (*Bezanty*).

Bordure Border round edge of shield.

Charge Device represented on shield.

Chevron Upturned V.

Chief The upper third of shield.

Couchant A beast lying on all fours.

Crest Device mounted on helmet and so depicted.

Demi or Demy Upper half of figure, animal etc.

Dexter Right (as opposed to Left, *Sinister*). In heraldic descriptions it is assumed that one is standing behind the shield, i.e. *Dexter* appears on the left to an onlooker.

Difference An addition or alteration to arms usually to make a distinction between otherwise identical arms.

Fess A band across the centre of a shield.

Field The background of a shield.

Fleur-de-lis Stylized lily.

Guardant Used of an animal looking out at the spectator.

Gules Red.

Impale To arrange two coats of arms side by side in one shield divided down the middle.

Label Horizontal bar usually with three or five points.

Leopard Heraldic lion *passant guardant*.

Lozenge Diamond shape, used to display a woman's arms.

Mantling Slashed cloth worn over helmet.

Modern Current arms, as opposed to *Ancient*.

Or Gold.

Pale Vertical stripe down shield. *Palewise*.

Passant Animal depicted walking, with foreleg raised.

Proper Depicted in natural colours.

Quarter To divide shield into four or more equal compartments.

Rampant Standing on one leg.

Sable Black.

Sinister Left as opposed to right
(*Dexter*).

Supporters Pair of figures on either side
of shield.

Vair Squirrel fur shown as stylized
pattern of blue and white.

Vert Green.

BIBLIOGRAPHY

Ailes, A., *The Origins of the Royal Arms of England* (1982).

Barnard, F. P., and Shepherd, T., *The Arms and Blasons of The Colleges of Oxford* (1929).

Boutell, Charles, *Boutell's Heraldry*, Revised ed. by J. P. Brooke-Little (1983).

Briggs, Geoffrey, *Civic and Corporate Heraldry* (1971).

Bromley, John, and Child, Heather, *The Armorial Bearings of the Guilds of London* (1960).

Child, Heather, *Heraldic Design* (1965).

Crosley, Richard, *London's Coats of Arms* (1928).

Dow, George, *Railway Heraldry* (1973).

Ellis, William Smith, *The Antiquities of Heraldry* (1869).

Eve, George W., *Decorative Heraldry: A Handbook of its Description and Treatment* (1908).

Fox-Davies, A. C., *A Complete Guide to Heraldry*, Revised ed. by J. P. Brooke-Little (1985).

Friar, Stephen, *A New Dictionary of Heraldry* (1987).

Hope, W. H. St. John, *Heraldry for Craftsmen and Designers* (1913).

London, H. S., *Royal Beasts* (1956).

Moncrieffe, I., and Pottinger, D., *Simple Heraldry* (1953).

Neubecker, O., *Heraldry, Sources, Symbols and Meaning* (1976).

Oldfield, R. W., *The Arms of the University and Colleges of Cambridge* (1931).

Parker, J., and Co., *Glossary of the Terms used in Heraldry* (1894).

Pinches, J. H. and R. V., *The Royal Heraldry of England* (1974).

Platts, B., *Origins of Heraldry* (1980).

Scott-Giles, C. W., *Civic Heraldry of England and Wales* (1933).

Scott-Giles, C. W., and Humphery-Smith, C., Peake, H., Wright, G. H., *A Cambridge Armorial* (1985).

Wagner, A. R., *Heralds of England* (1967).

Wagner, A. R., *Historic Heraldry of Britain* (1939).

Whittington, Betty, *Short History of the Royal Warrant* (1961).

Willement, T., *Regal Heraldry* (1821).

Woodcock, Thomas, and Robinson, John Martin, *The Oxford Guide to Heraldry* (1988).